# SISTERS

## BETTER TOGETHER

### ALICE & DORIS LIEU

WORKMAN PUBLISHING · NEW YORK

Library of Congress Cataloging-in-Publication Data is available.

ISBN 978-1-5235-1123-5

Design by Janet Vicario

Workman books are available at special discounts when purchased in
bulk for premiums and sales promotions as well as for fundraising or
educational use. Special editions or book excerpts can also be created
to specification. For details, contact the Special Sales Director at
specialmarkets@workman.com.

Workman Publishing Co., Inc.
225 Varick Street
New York, NY 10014-4381
workman.com

WORKMAN is a registered trademark of Workman Publishing Co., Inc.

Printed in China
First printing June 2021

10 9 8 7 6 5 4 3 2 1

**For Mom and Dad.**

Without the two of you, and your decision to keep the

"happy accident," aka Doris, this book would literally not

be possible! We are forever grateful for all that you do.

**And for Sparky,**

the pep in our step always; thank you for walking at least

one of us twice a day while we worked on this project.

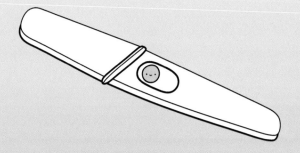

# INTRODUCTION

**Greetings! We are Alice and Doris, sisters born two years apart,** though friends and acquaintances alike are often surprised to discover that we are sisters since we hang out together so much. We are blessed to be able to stand a great deal of one another. This superpower of ours comes in handy, as ten years ago we launched our stationery company, ILOOTPAPERIE, and now we work out of our home studio, where pun-filled illustrations spring to life and there are many late nights spent hand-packing cards and other goods with care.

As sisters who live and work together, we have absolutely had our share of big laughs, impromptu dance parties in the wee hours of the morning, and, of course, epic fights and equally epic meltdowns. Yet we still genuinely look forward to spending more time together.

Although we weren't as close growing up as we are now, we have always considered ourselves incredibly lucky to have one another as we navigate both the good and bad phases of our lives. Whether it's going off course on a snowmobile during a blizzard on top of a glacier in Iceland and having to wait for the tour guides to come fetch us via GPS, or deep sea fishing in New Jersey where they boated us out beyond the point of an immediate return to shore and we fished until 6 a.m. to keep the waves of seasickness at bay (so! many! fish guts!), we have had many adventures together, all made infinitely better by having one another to lean on in uncertain times or relish the comical situations we get ourselves into. In both work and play, everything feels possible because we know we can figure it out together.

This project has been no different than our other life adventures, and it is definitely one for the books! It has also been such a gratifying and intense process for us to rigorously explore our own relationship and the universal truths of the sister bond (soul sisters included). We hope that when you read this book, you and your sister(s) are inspired to do the same: to take a pause and reflect on the countless things in your own lives that have been made better in the company of a sister.

xx Alice and Doris

# A SISTER IS...

a sidekick,

an accomplice,

and a sometime nemesis.

# TYPES OF
# SISTERS

**sorority sisters**

**sisters-in-law**

**teammates**

**nuns**

"For there is no friend like a sister
in calm or stormy weather;
To cheer one on the tedious way,
To fetch one if one goes astray,
To lift one if one totters down,
To strengthen whilst one stands."

—*Christina Rossetti*

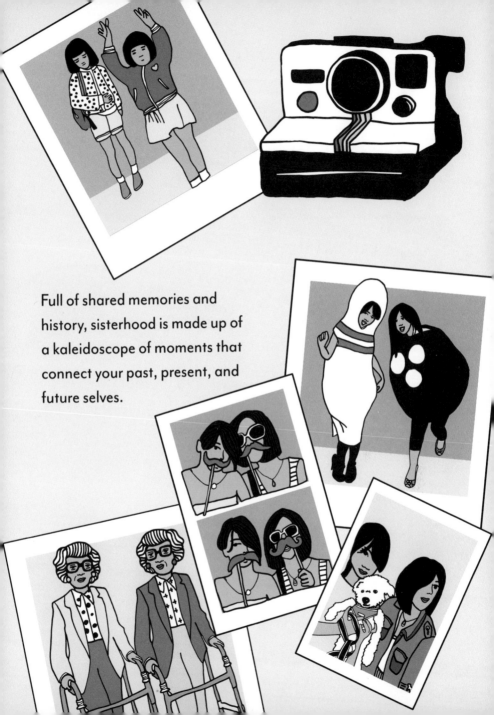

Full of shared memories and history, sisterhood is made up of a kaleidoscope of moments that connect your past, present, and future selves.

# A SISTER IS...

SOMEONE WHO
BELIEVES IN YOU!

(EVEN IF YOU DON'T QUITE
BELIEVE IN YOURSELF YET.)

car karaoke and spontaneous dance parties!

# THE BEST THINGS ABOUT
## BEING SISTERS

Laughing at each other's surprise
burps and farts

Ordering extra onions and garlic
without thinking twice

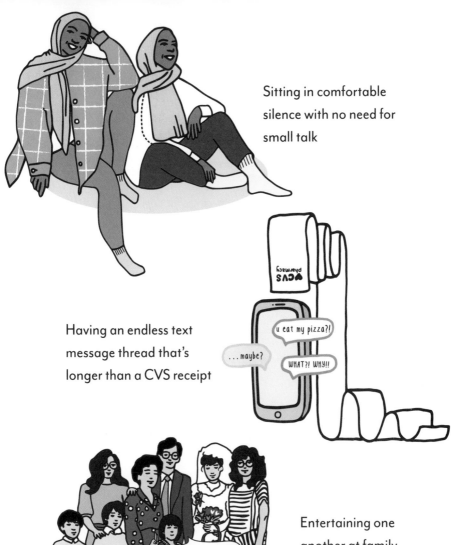

Sitting in comfortable silence with no need for small talk

Having an endless text message thread that's longer than a CVS receipt

Entertaining one another at family events

15

# A SISTER IS...

THE FIRST PERSON YOU WANT TO TELL WHEN THINGS GO RIGHT AND ALSO WHEN THINGS GO SOUTH.

# CONGRATS, SISTER!

**Fill in the blanks in the greeting below to toast your sister on a job well done.**

Hip hip hooooray, _____!
*(nickname)*

You are _____! Kudos to you on showing that _____ who's boss!
*(complimentary adjective)* *(noun)*

I knew you could do it, but you really kicked some major _____!
*(body part)*

I am so proud of you for all the _____ and _____ you have put in
*(noun)* *(noun)*

these past few _____. Let's break out a couple bottles of _____,
*(time frame)* *(drink of choice)*

put on some party _____, and get this _____ shindig started!
*(article of clothing)* *(adjective)*

Can't wait to give you a _____!
*(noun)*

Chest bump!

_____
*(your name)*

YOU
ROCK!

# IF YOU WERE CAMPING IN THE MOUNTAINS, SHE WOULD BE...

the campfire, providing warmth and good company on cold nights.

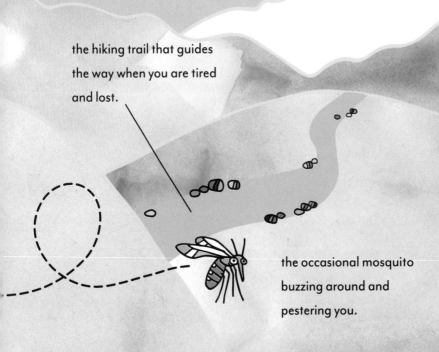

the hiking trail that guides
the way when you are tired
and lost.

the occasional mosquito
buzzing around and
pestering you.

the pebble that sometimes
gets into your hiking boot,
rubbing you the wrong way.

19

# PIONEERING SISTERS

### Queen Mary I and Queen Elizabeth I

Mary was England's first "queen regnant," a monarch who rules the country in her own right, not as the mother or wife of another person. After Mary died, her half sister, Elizabeth, was crowned Queen of England, and her forty-four-year reign became known as a golden age in English history. They are buried together in Westminster Abbey, where the Latin inscription on their monument reads: "Partners in throne and grave, here we sleep Elizabeth and Mary, sisters in [the] hope of the Resurrection."

### Emily and Elizabeth Blackwell

In 1849, Elizabeth became the first woman to receive a medical degree in the United States, and together the sisters founded the first women-run hospital in the nation in 1857.

### The Hyers Sisters

Classically trained singers Anna Madah and Emma Louise Hyers were among the first Black women to tour the United States as concert artists. They toured from 1871 to 1894, performing traditional European music, but later transitioned to producing and starring in some of the earliest civil rights musical plays that emphasized the dignity and humanity of Black people to counteract the degrading caricatures often depicted in minstrel shows and entertainment of that era.

## Tatyana and Hannah McFadden

In 2012, Tatyana and Hannah became the first siblings to compete against each other at the Paralympic Games in London.

## Tashi and Nungshi Malik

In 2013, the Malik sisters earned a Guinness World Record for being the first twin sisters to climb Mount Everest. They are also the first twins and the youngest people to complete the Explorers Grand Slam, climbing the world's seven highest peaks and skiing to the North and South Poles.

## Shoni and Jude Schimmel

The Schimmel sisters played basketball together at the University of Louisville and helped lead the team to the women's NCAA championship finals in 2013. They electrified fans with a style of play called rez ball (short for reservation ball, which they grew up playing on the Umatilla Reservation in Oregon). They were also the subjects of the basketball documentary *Off the Rez*.

## Linda Sánchez and Loretta Sanchez

The first and, so far, only sisters to serve in Congress together, Linda and Loretta both served as representatives of California. Their terms overlapped from 2003 to 2017.

WHEN YOU SAY YOU'RE NOT GOING TO TELL
ANYONE, YOUR SISTER DOESN'T COUNT.

# A SISTER IS...

someone with whom you can
be your true self, flaws and all.
(No point in hiding them—
she knows!)

# SISTER MOVIES

## WE LOVE

SISTER ACT

A League OF THEIR OWN

# THE THREE SISTERS

The Three Sisters—or De-o-ha-ko, a name given by the Iroquois people of North America—farming method was developed in ancient Mesoamerica as a way to ensure that the three main agricultural crops—beans, corn, and squash, the "Three Sisters"—flourished by planting them together.

The cornstalks provide support for the beans to grow.

The beans pull nitrogen from the air into the soil while also growing through the squash vines and winding their way up the cornstalks into the sunlight, holding the sisters close together.

The large and prickly squash leaves help protect the trio from animals, pests, and even weeds, while also creating shade to keep the soil cool and moist.

# BETTER TOGETHER

waiting in line

# A SISTER IS...

someone who doesn't mind
listening to your stories over
and over again, because you
do the same for her.

CHLOE X HALLE

THE KIM LOO SISTERS

THE KIM SISTERS

PLAY IT ON REPEAT!

"Sisters annoy, interfere,
criticize. Indulge in monumental
sulks, in huffs, in snide remarks.
Borrow. Break. Monopolize
the bathroom. Are always underfoot.
But sisters are your second self.
And if catastrophe should strike,
sisters are there.
Defending you against
all corners."

—*Pam Brown*

# THE BEST THINGS ABOUT
## BEING SISTERS

Asking each other personal questions and sharing stories that others would think are TMI

Stalking exes and crushes on social media together with no shame

JOMO: the joy of missing out on other plans to have spur-of-the-moment slumber parties

Learning from each other's mistakes

# ON BORROWING CLOTHES

**THE DREAM:** Borrowing clothes and "shopping" in her closet

ADD TO CART!

ADD TO CART!

ADD TO CART!

**THE REALITY:** Items may be "borrowed" indefinitely or returned with stains, leading to epic showdowns

# SISTER ACTS

### The Andrews Sisters

LaVerne, Maxene, and Patty Andrews made up a close harmony trio during the swing and boogie-woogie era, and their style and songs continue to influence entertainers such as Bette Midler and Christina Aguilera. They sold more than 100 million records, and their career spanned over five decades.

### The Pointer Sisters

The Pointer Sisters started as a duo with June and Bonnie but eventually became a quartet when Anita and Ruth joined. They went on to win three Grammy Awards and had thirteen US top 20 hits between 1973 and 1985, including "Jump (For My Love)" and "He's So Shy."

### HAIM

Este, Danielle, and Alana Haim are the three sisters who make up the Los Angeles pop rock band HAIM, formed in 2007. In 2018, the trio embarked on their second headlining tour (Sister Sister Sister Tour), with thirty-seven stops across the United States and Europe.

## Sister Sledge

Sisters Debbie, Joni, Kim, and Kathy formed the band Sister Sledge in 1971, and their hit "We Are Family" earned a Grammy nomination for Best R&B Vocal Performance by a Duo, Group or Chorus in 1979.

## Heart

Ann and Nancy Wilson are the lead vocalists of the rock band Heart, formed in 1970. In 2013, they were inducted into the Rock & Roll Hall of Fame, where they are recognized as the first women to front a hard rock band.

## Tegan and Sara

Tegan and Sara Quin are identical twin sisters who formed their indie pop band in 1998 and have since released nine studio albums. As openly gay advocates for LGBTQ+ equality, they founded the Tegan and Sara Foundation in 2016 to fight for the rights and representation of LGBTQ+ girls and women.

## The Clark Sisters

With the help of their mother, Mattie Moss Clark, a prolific gospel singer and choir director, the Clark Sisters (Jacky, Denise, Elbernita "Twinkie," Dorinda, and Karen) became the top-selling women gospel group of all time and are often credited with changing the sound of modern gospel music.

41

"If you don't annoy your big sister for no good reason from time to time, she thinks you don't love her anymore."

—*Pearl Cleage*

# Most Annoying
# Sister Certificate

THIS CERTIFICATE RECOGNIZES

_____

*(name of honoree)*

FOR BEING THE MOST ANNOYING SISTER EVER ON

_____

*(date and year)*

BY VIRTUE OF OUR AUTHORITY,

WITH ALL THE HONORS, RIGHTS, AND

PRIVILEGES THERETO PERTAINING.

**200%**
**AUTHENTICALLY**
**CERTIFIED**

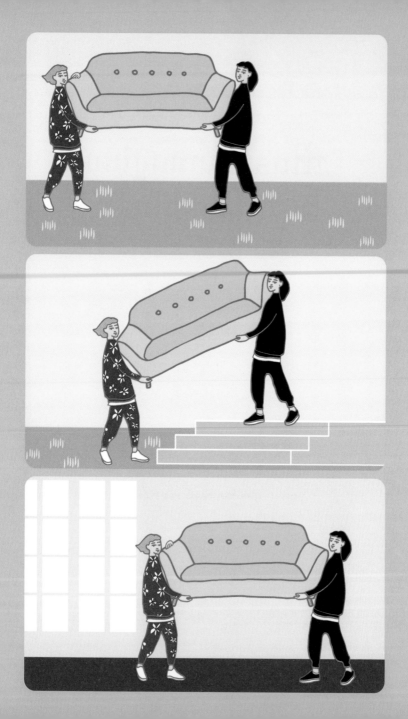

# A SISTER IS...

your teammate for life.

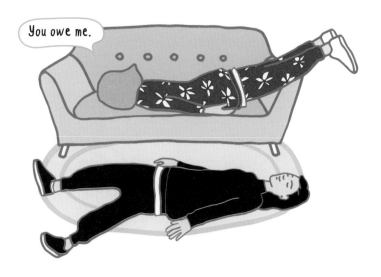

# THINGS ONLY A SISTER KNOWS

**TOP SECRET** CLASSIFIED

1. How to push your buttons in the most infuriating way possible

2. An inside joke that makes you both burst into a fit of laughter without either of you saying a word

3. Your wild ambitions and dreams that you aren't ready to share with the rest of the world

4. When you say you don't mind something, but you actually do

5. All of your most embarrassing and cringeworthy moments

6. The trouble you've gotten into that your parents never found out about

7. The off-the-Richter-scale tantrums you've thrown in private

THINGS ONLY A SISTER KNOWS

TOP SECRET

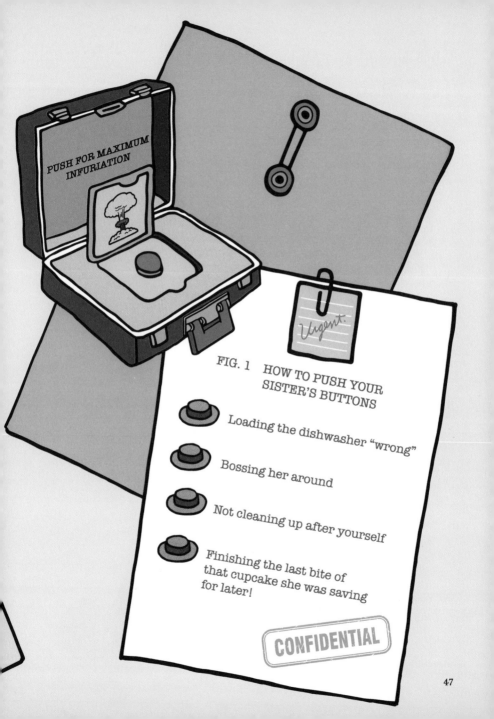

47

# WHEN YOU'RE HAVING A ROUGH DAY, SHE SENDS YOU CUTE PUPPY / CAT / OTHER ANIMAL VIDEOS TO CHEER YOU UP.

# VENUS AND EARTH

Venus is known as Earth's sister planet, or twin, because of their similarities in size, mass, and composition. Of all the planets, Venus is the closest in size to Earth, with a mass roughly equivalent to 80 percent of Earth's and a diameter that is only a few miles less than Earth's. Their size and density suggest they share a similar internal structure: a core, mantle, and crust. However, Venus is also sometimes referred to as Earth's "twisted sister" because of some stark differences that make the planet uninhabitable. For example, Venus lacks a strong magnetic field that would help protect the planet from exposure to high amounts of radiation from the sun.

Venus

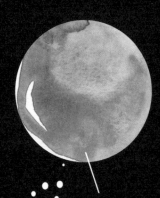

Earth

"I grew up believing my sister was from the planet Neptune and had been sent down to Earth to kill me."

—Zooey Deschanel

# ON COMPETITION AND COMPARISON

**THE REALITY:** You are naturally measured against one another. Growing up, you often competed for attention, fighting to be seen and to establish your own identities.

**THE FLIP SIDE:** This sense of competition can allow you to become each other's biggest advocate, as you both grow and defy the labels others put on you.

# WHEN SISTERS FIGHT

**START HERE!**

ACID RAIN

**Step 5:** You both cool off, but you both still believe you're right.

**Step 6:** You put the fight on pause and go back to normal because there's something you really need to tell her.

**Step 7:** Repeat steps 1–6.

**Step 1:** She intentionally pushes your buttons.

MANTLE

**Step 4:** You try to talk it out, but emotions erupt and you find yourselves arguing again.

ERUPTION CLOUD

LAVA FLOW

VOLCANIC BOMBS

**Step 3:** You stop speaking to each other. Tension builds.

CONTINENTAL CRUST

**Step 2:** You push her buttons right back!

OCEANIC CRUST

MAGMA CHAMBER

# SOMETIMES IT'S BETTER TO BE APART...

AND THAT'S OK TOO.

# SISTER RIVALRIES

### Olivia de Havilland and Joan Fontaine

Spurred by a childhood rivalry, Olivia and Joan both became successful actresses during Hollywood's Golden Age. They were the first pair of siblings to compete against each other for Best Actress at the Academy Awards in 1942 and also the only siblings to win Best Actor/Actress (Olivia in 1947 and Joan in 1942).

### Venus and Serena Williams

Venus and Serena Williams have faced off against each other thirty times in professional tournaments over two decades. Although Venus dominated the first few years of their matches, Serena holds the most wins (18–12). Despite their competitive rivalry on the court, their bond remains intensely close.

## The Soong Sisters

The three Soong sisters, Ei-ling, Ching-ling, and May-ling (who became Madame Chiang Kai-Shek), were direct and influential participants in the twentieth-century struggle between Nationalists and Communists that helped shape China into the country it is today. Their differing beliefs led May-ling and Ei-ling to pledge their allegiance to the Nationalist party, while Ching-ling supported and worked with the Communist party. As a consequence, the sisters became estranged after 1949, never to meet all together again.

## Esther and Pauline Friedman

Esther "Eppie" and Pauline "Popo" Friedman were identical twins who both had syndicated advice columns in national newspapers. Although Pauline initially helped Esther when she landed the "Ann Landers" column, the *Chicago Sun-Times* prohibited a partnership, prompting Pauline to start the "Dear Abby" column for the *San Francisco Chronicle*.

## Jacqueline Kennedy Onassis and Caroline Lee Radziwill

Caroline Lee Radziwill often felt overshadowed by her older sister, former first lady Jacqueline Kennedy Onassis, although both women were known as style icons. They competed for their parents' affections and were at times drawn to the same men, making for a complicated sisterhood tinged with jealousy and strife.

# I'M SORRY, SISTER!

**Fill in the blanks in the greeting below to offer a sincere apology (with a side of humor) to your sister.**

Dear_____,
(sister's name)

I am _____ about our little tiff over _____. I hope you are able to see
(adjective)                                              (noun)

past my _____ _____ because I only want the _____
(adjective)        (noun)                                              (noun)

for you!  You mean the _____ to me, and I don't know what's tighter—our
(noun)

_____ or our relationship—but I cherish them both! Let's please
(article of clothing)

_____ it out and make up already—I have a backlog of _____
(verb)                                                                            (adjective)

_____ that I've been _____ to share with you!
(noun)                              (verb-ing)

Your very _____ sister,
(adjective)

_____
(your name)

# PEACE OFFERINGS

Lots of bread

Surprise spa day

Spaghetti dinner

Freshly baked cookies

Flowers

MY BAD.

Humorous greeting card

Fried chicken

A new houseplant

Surprise
delivery

"We'll always fight, but we'll always make up as well. That's what sisters do: we argue, we point out each other's frailties, mistakes, and bad judgment, we flash the insecurities we've had since childhood, and then we come back together. Until the next time."

—*Lisa See*

# BETTER TOGETHER

## adventures big and small

### ① Sisters, Oregon

The city of Sisters is known as the Gateway to the Cascades and takes its name from the Three Sisters mountains (three closely spaced volcanic peaks called North Sister, Middle Sister, and South Sister) located in the Deschutes National Forest.

### ② Seven Sisters Oak (Mandeville, Louisiana)

The largest live oak tree registered by the Live Oak Society. It is estimated to be around 1,200 years old and was originally called Doby's Seven Sisters since it is located on the property once owned by the Doby family and Mrs. Doby was one of seven sisters.

### 3 Systrafoss (Kirkjubæjarklaustur, Iceland)

Icelandic for Sister's Falls and named after the Benedictine nuns who lived together in the small town of Kirkjubæjarklaustur, where the falls are located. The falls are fed by the overflow from Systravatn (Sister's Lake).

### 4 Seven Sisters Cliffs (East Sussex, England)

A series of chalk cliffs along the English Channel, with seven separate crests that make up the cliffs' profile. The cliffs have appeared in various movies, including *Harry Potter and the Goblet of Fire* and *Atonement*.

### 5 Seven Sisters of India

Northeast India is comprised of seven states: Arunachal Pradesh, Assam, Meghalaya, Manipur, Mizoram, Nagaland, and Tripura. Isolated from the tourist circuit, they are also known as "Paradise Unexplored" as they share similar majestic geographical features that are the least explored of India.

# Secrets Sisters Share

## . . . IF WE TOLD YOU, WE WOULD HAVE TO KILL YOU!

"Don't talk about my
sister; don't play with me
about my sister. If you do,
you'll see another
side of me."

—*Beyoncé Knowles*

# NOW PLAYING

## SISTERS DOUBLE FEATURE

*A Beautiful Mess*
## ELSIE & EMMA

## NOVA & MARIGOLD

## STARRING . . .
## ELSIE LARSON AND EMMA CHAPMAN

In 2007, Elsie Larson started a DIY blog called *A Beautiful Mess*, where she shared crafts, home decor, and personal moments. Over the past fourteen years, Elsie, her sister, Emma, and their team have turned the site into a lifestyle company in addition to writing three books and creating multiple apps.

**Elsie on Emma:** "So this [2010] is really the year Emma and I started to blog together and I asked her to become a coauthor with me. Since then we have done everything together and owned everything 50/50. By far the best decision of my life."

**Emma on Elsie:** "I love having her in meetings. . . . She makes me excited to reach farther than I think I ever would without her, and I think she inspires other people to do that too."

## STARRING . . .
## NOVA AND MARIGOLD LARSON

*A Beautiful Mess* also became a platform on which Elsie and her husband, Jeremy, shared their journey to adopt Nova Winter Larson, a two-year-old girl with albinism, from China.

After a year and a half with Nova, Elsie and Jeremy adopted Marigold June, giving each girl the gift of a sister who looks similar to her and plays at the same pace due to their limited vision, instilling in both an invaluable sense of belonging.

# THE SEVEN SISTERS

## SAN FRANCISCO, CALIFORNIA

This iconic row of seven houses in Alamo Square, famous for appearing in the opening credits of *Full House*, is known as the "Seven Sisters" on Postcard Row. Built by Matthew Kavanaugh between 1892 and 1896, the houses are the most popular of San Francisco's "Painted Ladies," Victorian houses that are painted with three or more colors and feature the Queen Anne architectural

style, including gingerbread-style gables, intricate stained glass paneling, painted classical columns, cutaway bay windows, and lacy decorative spindlework. The bright, cheerful colors of the Seven Sisters were inspired by the Colorist Movement, which began in the 1960s and was led by local San Francisco artist Butch Kardum.

**PRO TIP FOR SIGHTSEERS:** In the second-to-last home, there is a tiny museum on the top floor that houses small tokens of historical San Francisco memorabilia, such as a ticket from the day the Golden Gate Bridge opened.

the sunshine on your face,
brightening the cloudiest
of days.

the reflection of the sun on the
water, at times making things
a little heated.

# IF YOU WERE SWIMMING IN THE OCEAN, SHE WOULD BE...

the sand that is everywhere and gets into everything.

your life jacket, keeping you afloat in rough seas.

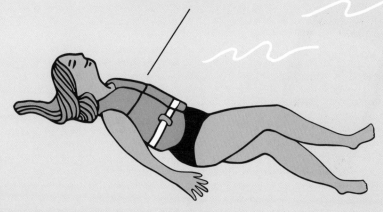

# A SISTER IS...

someone who helps you put sunblock on the hard-to-reach spots and tells you when you've got white streaks all over your face.

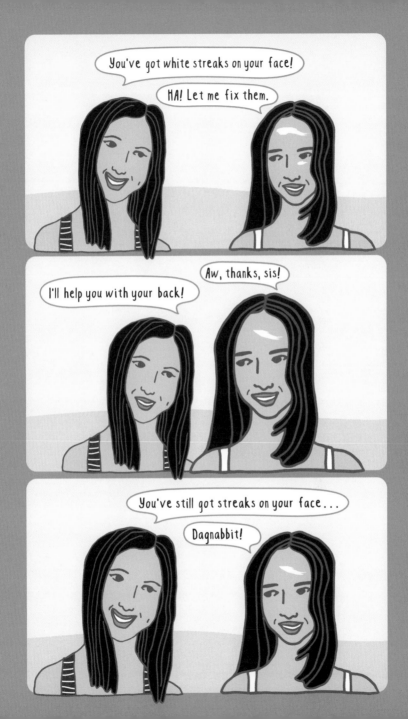

# BETTER TOGETHER

scary movies (if you get scared
witless, you can keep each other
company all night with the lights on,
no judgment!)

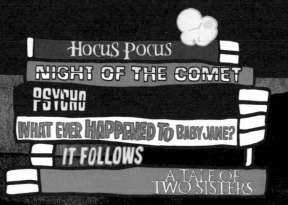

HOCUS POCUS

NIGHT OF THE COMET

PSYCHO

WHAT EVER HAPPENED TO BABY JANE?

IT FOLLOWS

A TALE OF TWO SISTERS

On-Screen Sisters

**Lillian and Dorothy Gish**
*(An Unseen Enemy)*

**Karisma and Kareena Kapoor**
Bollywood Stars

**Cardi B and Hennessy**
*(Love & Hip Hop: New York)*

**Tia and Tamera Mowry**
*(Sister, Sister)*

**Eva, Magda, and Zsa Zsa Gabor**
Actresses and Socialites

**Lisa and Louise Burns**
*(The Shining)*

**Dakota and Elle Fanning**
*(I Am Sam)*

# A SISTER IS...

someone who remembers your likes and dislikes even better than you do (and sometimes uses this information to get what she wants).

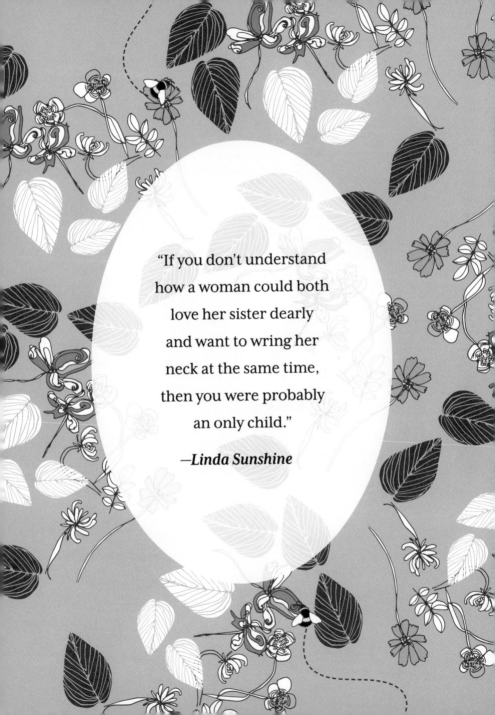

"If you don't understand
how a woman could both
love her sister dearly
and want to wring her
neck at the same time,
then you were probably
an only child."

—*Linda Sunshine*

# YOUR SISTER IS MOST ANNOYING WHEN SHE:

## MEMO

- ☑ Calls you out on your bullshit.
- ◯ Gets into your business and tells you what to do.
- ◯ Is in the bathroom when you need to use it.
- ◯ Gives you pesky nicknames that stick.
- ☑ Pushes your buttons on purpose.
- ◯ Gets away with something you can't.

# YOU BOTH GET ANNOYED WHEN OTHER PEOPLE:

## MEMO

- ◯ Mix up your names.

- ☑ Tell you how much you look like one another, when you look nothing alike!

- ◯ Ask (or assume) who is older.

- ◯ Refer to you as "so and so's older sister" or "so and so's younger sister."

- ◯ Talk to you to get information on your sister.

- ◯ Blame you for something your sister did.

# SHE KNOWS ALL YOUR CRUSHES!

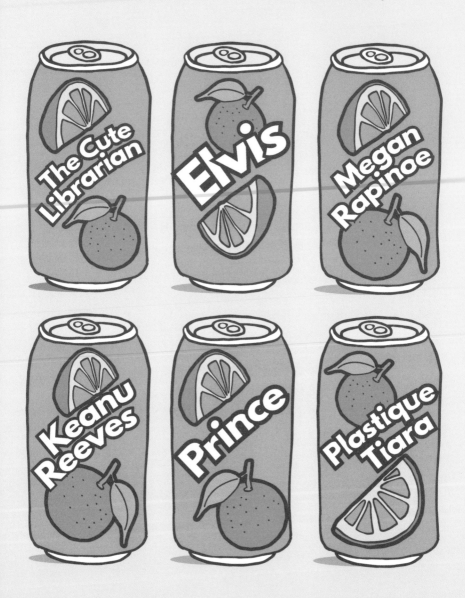

# BETTER TOGETHER

making tough decisions and solving problems (because two brains—or more!— are definitely better than one)

$$\frac{5x + 5y + 5z}{F(x)}$$

best way to get over a breakup

how to navigate office politics

what's for dinner?

# A SISTER IS...

a built-in backup system.

**Nikki Bella and Brie Bella** (aka The Bella Twins) are identical twin sisters who were once a professional wrestling tag team.

# BOOKS ABOUT SISTERS

| TITLE | AUTHOR |
|-------|--------|
| Beezus and Ramona | Beverly Cleary |
| The Vanishing Half | Brit Bennett |
| To All the Boys I've Loved Before | Jenny Han |
| The Lives and Loves of Daisy and Violet Hilton | Dean Jensen |
| Pride and Prejudice | Jane Austen |
| How the García Girls Lost Their Accents | Julia Alvarez |
| The Blind Assassin | Margaret Atwood |
| Like Water for Chocolate | Laura Esquivel |
| In Her Shoes | Jennifer Weiner |
| My Sister's Keeper | Jodi Picoult |
| The God of Small Things | Arundhati Roy |
| Homegoing | Yaa Gyasi |
| Little Women | Louisa May Alcott |

PUBLIC LIBRARY

## ON GROWING UP

**THEN:** She was the tattletale who always got you in trouble.

**NOW:** She's your partner in crime and even at times your alibi.

# HEROIC SISTERS

### Trung Trac and Trung Nhi

Sisters Trung Trac and Trung Nhi led the first Vietnamese independence movement in 39 CE and established a brief matriarchal independent state.

### Angelina Grimké Weld and Sarah Grimké

Angelina Grimké Weld and her sister, Sarah, were prominent abolitionists and women's rights activists. They became the first women agents of the American Anti-Slavery Society during a time when society disapproved of women speaking to audiences of men and women in public.

### Stefania and Helena Podgorska

During the Holocaust, Stefania Podgorska and her younger sister, Helena, successfully hid and saved thirteen Jews in the attic of their home in Poland.

## Patria, Minerva, and María Teresa Mirabal

Patria, Minerva, and María Teresa Mirabal (Las Mariposas) are considered national heroines in the Dominican Republic for their opposition to dictator Rafael Trujillo and the part they played in the eventual restoration of democracy in their nation.

## Melati and Isabel Wijsen

In 2013, sisters Melati and Isabel, ages 12 and 10, founded their social campaign, Bye Bye Plastic Bags, in their homeland of Bali, Indonesia, one of the world's largest plastic polluters. Their organization fights for environmental education and eradication of plastic bags throughout the world.

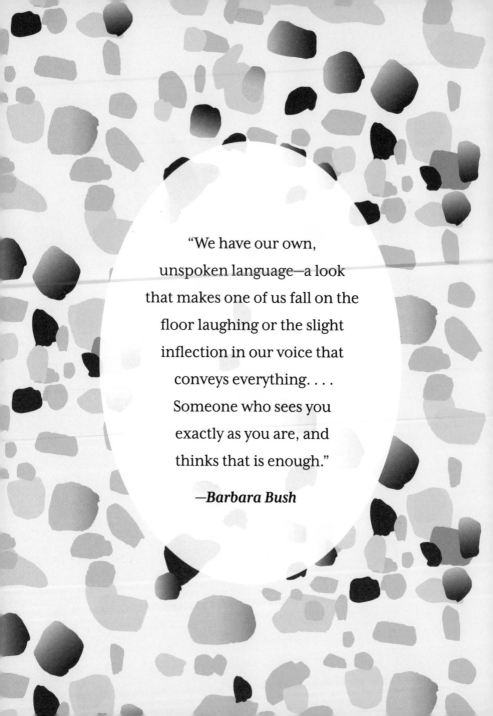

"We have our own,
unspoken language—a look
that makes one of us fall on the
floor laughing or the slight
inflection in our voice that
conveys everything. . . .
Someone who sees you
exactly as you are, and
thinks that is enough."

—*Barbara Bush*

# BETTER TOGETHER

growing old and reminiscing about
past antics and daydreaming
about future adventures

ONWARD! XX

# POWERHOUSE SISTERS

### Flo and Kay Lyman

Flo and Kay Lyman are the world's only women identical twin autistic savants (people on the autism spectrum who have astounding skills in a specific area). Both twins can state the day of the week for any date and are able to recall the weather and what they ate on any day of their lives.

### Beyoncé and Solange Knowles

Both multitalented superstars in their own right, Beyoncé Knowles and her younger sister, Solange, have achieved commercial and critical acclaim over the years and are the first sisters to both have albums that debuted at No. 1 on the Billboard charts.

### The Brontë Sisters

Charlotte, Emily, and Anne Brontë grew up playing games and telling stories based on complex imaginary worlds that helped foster their passion for the written word. All three sisters went on to publish novels that are now considered masterpieces: Charlotte's *Jane Eyre*, Emily's *Wuthering Heights*, and Anne's *The Tenant of Wildfell Hall*.

## Laura and Kate Mulleavy

Designers Laura and Kate Mulleavy are the creators and founders of Rodarte, an award-winning fashion line that is renowned for its meticulous handiwork. The initial collection of just ten pieces launched them onto the cover of *Women's Wear Daily* and secured the sisters a meeting with *Vogue*'s editor-in-chief Anna Wintour.

## Mary-Kate and Ashley Olsen

Mary-Kate and Ashley Olsen landed their acting debut as Michelle Tanner in *Full House* when they were just nine months old. They went on to become copresidents of their entertainment company, Dualstar Entertainment Group, at the age of eighteen, but eventually turned their focus to fashion, launching multiple collections that include award-winning The Row and Elizabeth and James.

## Lana and Lilly Wachowski

Lana and Lilly Wachowski are trans women directors, writers, and producers who have often worked as a team. Their second film, *The Matrix*, achieved major box office success and won four Academy Awards; in 2012, it was selected for preservation in the National Film Registry by the Library of Congress for being "culturally, historically, and aesthetically significant."

# IF YOU WERE EXPLORING IN THE ARCTIC, SHE WOULD BE...

the occasional blustery wind that you must fight against to get where you want to go.

the snow fox that sneaks up on you and swoops in to steal the food you've caught in your traps.

the wool mittens and socks that keep you warm and toasty.

your snowshoes, keeping you from sinking in the snow.

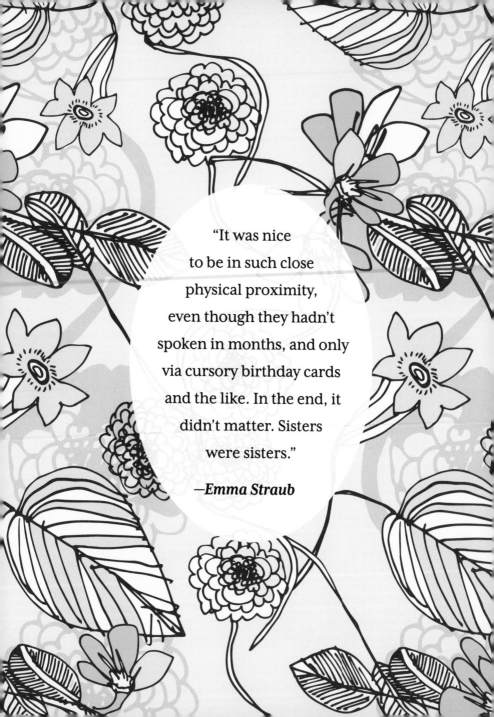

"It was nice to be in such close physical proximity, even though they hadn't spoken in months, and only via cursory birthday cards and the like. In the end, it didn't matter. Sisters were sisters."

—*Emma Straub*

# HAPPY BIRTHDAY, SISTER!

**Fill in the blanks in the greeting below to liven up your birthday wishes for your sister.**

Dearest _____!
        *(affectionate nickname)*

Get ready to put on your birthday _____! Because we are going to _____
                        *(article of clothing)*                    *(verb)*

the night away and have loads of _____ _____ to properly ring in this
                            *(adjective)*    *(noun)*

occasion! You are the _____ beneath my wings and the _____ to
                    *(noun)*                            *(condiment)*

my _____! _____ is always better with you (although remember the
    *(food)*        *(noun)*

time you _____ my favorite _____ ??). This year is gonna be
        *(verb, past tense)*        *(noun)*

_____—can't wait to go on more _____ with my favorite
    *(adjective)*                        *(plural noun)*

person in the universe! Have a happy _____ birthday!
                                *(adjective)*

With all my _____,
            *(noun)*

_____
    *(your name)*

# A SISTER IS...

someone you look forward to making plans with, even if you see them every day.

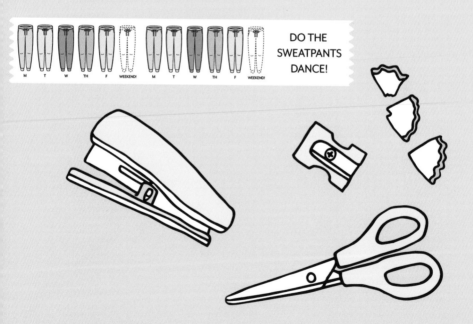

DO THE SWEATPANTS DANCE!

 **NOVEMBER**

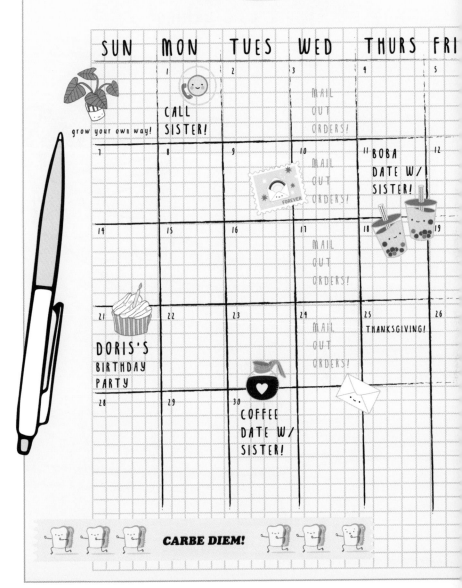

| SUN | MON | TUES | WED | THURS | FRI |
|-----|-----|------|-----|-------|-----|
| *grow your own way!* | 1 CALL SISTER! | 2 | 3 MAIL OUT ORDERS! | 4 | 5 |
| 7 | 8 | 9 | 10 MAIL OUT ORDERS! | 11 BOBA DATE W/ SISTER! | 12 |
| 14 | 15 | 16 | 17 MAIL OUT ORDERS! | 18 | 19 |
| 21 DORIS'S BIRTHDAY PARTY | 22 | 23 | 24 MAIL OUT ORDERS! | 25 THANKSGIVING! | 26 |
| 28 | 29 | 30 COFFEE DATE W/ SISTER! | | | |

*CARBE DIEM!*

# BETTER TOGETHER

*simply everything!*

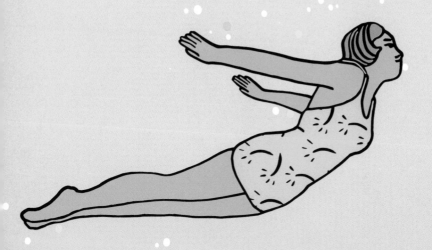

Good days are better when shared, and even when some days downright suck and you can't see through the mud, knowing that you have your sister in your corner gives you peace of mind and allows you the freedom to launch more fearlessly into the world.

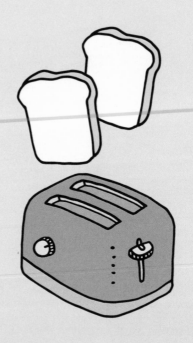

# ACKNOWLEDGMENTS

HUZZAH! WE MADE IT! And we really couldn't have without all of you . . . so here's a toast!

A big cheer goes out to Mom and Dad for your steadfast support of our adventures with ILOOTPAPERIE, including this book project, over the years. We so very much appreciate both your helping hands and graceful understanding as we navigate through busy seasons and this year: book deadlines! Thank you, Mom, for being our #1 fan from day one and for the cut garden roses on those days we needed the extra deadline JIA YO mojo! And Dad, for your power card-packing prowess that never fails to astonish us and gets us through those intense order deadlines!

We are so grateful to Rachael Mt. Pleasant, our fearless editor, Janet Vicario, Hillary Leary, Julie Primavera, Terri Wowk, Moira Kerrigan, Kate Oksen, Claire Gross, and the rest of the team at Workman Publishing, for giving us the opportunity and trusting us to handle this dream project with care. It truly takes a village. Thank you, Rachael, for your unwavering patience through this daunting journey and those little nudges that led us to uncover more sister gems to share, not to mention meticulously combing through each page with us (multiple times!) to help shape the book to be its best self. And kudos to Janet, our book designer, who kept us on our toes with her technical knowledge of all things graphic design!

To our community of creatives, stockists, and fellow snail mail pun lovers and friends—thank you all for being a part of this magic! It is because of you that we have been able to continue this endeavor for the past 10+ years that led us to this project, and we thank you for coming along with us on this truly wild, wild ride.

Last but not least: Thank you, Universe! We feel sure that someone out there must be listening to all our secret hopes and dreams. Please keep it coming!

**FANCIFUL DAYDREAMS ARE BETTER TOGETHER.**

Sisters Alice and Doris Lieu are the founders of ILOOTPAPERIE, a stationery company fueled by their love of paper goods, funny drawings, and a keen appreciation for puns. Their products can be found in Urban Outfitters, Paper Source, and more than 200 independent retailers across the country. With their pup Sparky in tow, Alice and Doris live and work out of their home studio in Pasadena, California.